My First Book of
VEGETABLES

KIRAN REKHA BANERJI

RED TURTLE
RUPA

Published in Red Turtle by
Rupa Publications India Pvt. Ltd 2017
7/16, Ansari Road, Daryaganj
New Delhi 110002

Sales centres:
Allahabad Bengaluru Chennai
Hyderabad Jaipur Kathmandu
Kolkata Mumbai

Text Copyright © Kiran Rekha Banerji 2017
Illustrations Copyright © Rupa Publications India Pvt. Ltd 2017
Design by Roy Creation

The views and opinions expressed in this book are the author's own and the facts are as reported by him/her which have been verified to the extent possible, and the publishers are not in any way liable for the same.

ISBN: 978-81-291-4557-4

First impression 2017

10 9 8 7 6 5 4 3 2 1

The moral right of the author has been asserted.

This book belongs to:

....

....

Potato

I am potato, the most common vegetable. I am pale white inside with a brown skin outside. I come in many shapes and sizes. I grow under the ground. Children like me most as fries and chips. I am available all the year round. I am a great source of energy for you and your family.

Green Bean

I am green bean. I am thin, long and soft. You can eat me with noodles, rice or chapatti. You can also add me to your soup. I am a rich source of vitamins and minerals which keep you in good health. I grow on a creeper.

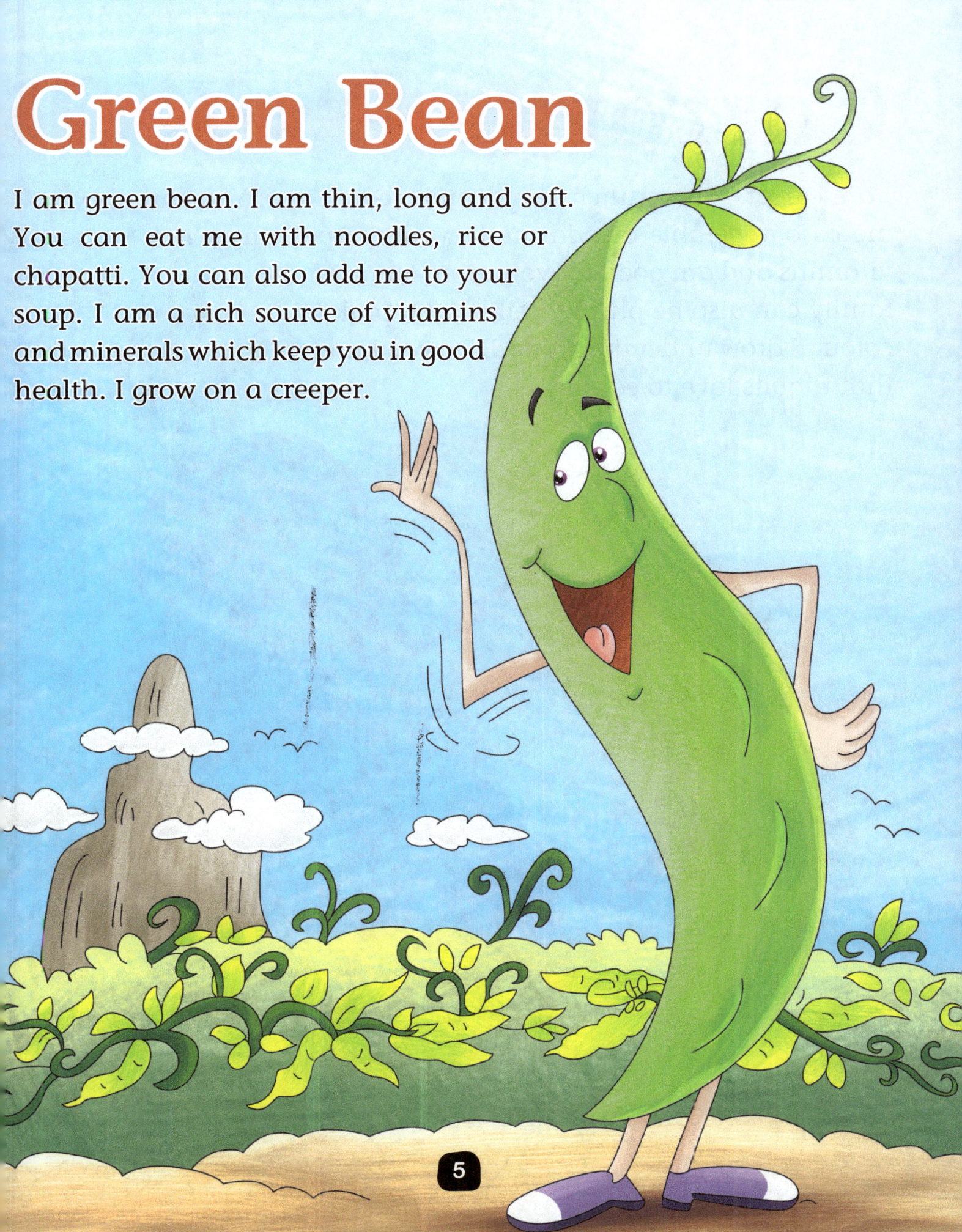

Carrot

I am carrot. I am crunchy and can be eaten raw. You can also cook me as a vegetable or add me to your soup. I am a rich source of vitamins and am good for your eyes. Some of my family can also be purple, yellow and pink in colour. I grow under the ground. Do you know that rabbits love to eat me?

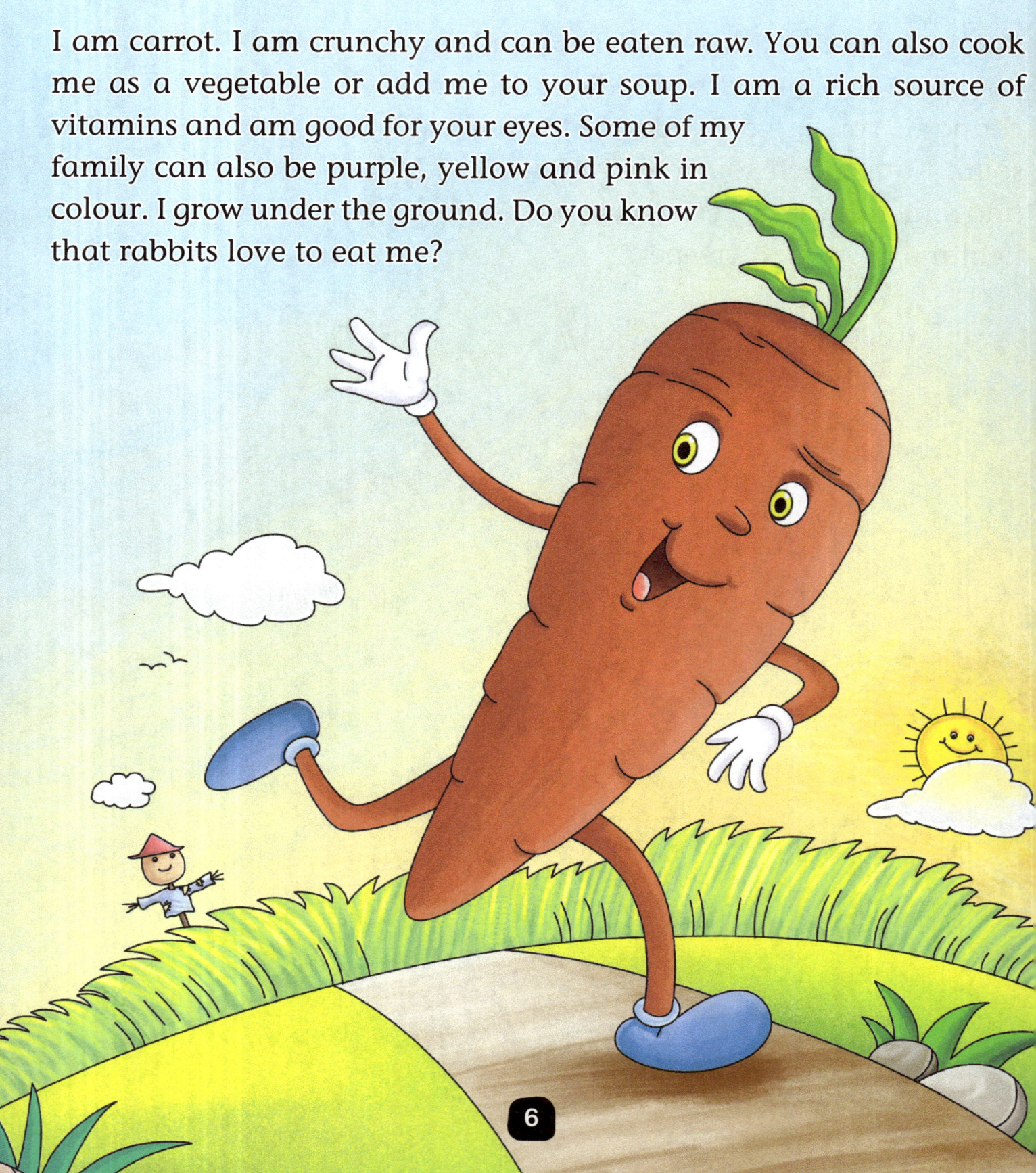

Cauliflower

I am cauliflower. I look like a white flower surrounded by big and small green leaves. You can eat me with rice or chapatti. I can also be added to your soup to make it tasty. I have plenty of minerals and vitamins to keep you healthy. Do you know where I grow?

Cucumber

I am cucumber, green and long. I am found in salads and can be eaten raw at any time. I can also be mixed with yoghurt to keep you cool in summer. I have plenty of minerals and vitamins to keep you healthy. I am easy to grow.

Cabbage

I am cabbage. I am a round bundle of many leaves tightly packed together. I have plenty of nutrients and I help you to stay healthy. I can be eaten raw in a salad. I can also be cooked in many ways. I am green, but my cousin is purple.

Capsicum

I am capsicum. I am green in colour, with a special smell and taste. I contain plenty of vitamins and keep diseases away. My cousins come in different colours. Some are red, yellow and orange. We are also known as bell peppers! Do you know that we belong to the chilli family?

Broccoli

I am broccoli. I look like a cauliflower but I am dark green in colour. Many children like me cooked in butter. I can also be made into tasty soups. I contain a large amount of minerals to help you grow strong. I am also one of the biggest sources of vitamin C.

Colocasia (arvi)

I am colocasia or arvi. I am also known as taro. I have large dark green leaves. I am dark brown in colour and have tiny hair on my skin. When peeled, I am pale white inside. I am sticky when boiled but I can also be cooked to become crisp. I grow underground in extremely wet areas.

Bottle gourd

I am called the bottle gourd because I look like a bottle. I have a light green skin. When the skin is peeled, I am soft and white inside. I am easy to digest. I can be mixed with cereals, lentils and can also be cooked as soup. I grow on a creeper. Do you know that my leaves can also be eaten?

Onion

I am onion. I am pink in colour with a crisp, papery skin. I have a strong smell. When sliced, you will find various layers within. I grow under the ground. If you peel and cut me, I bring tears to your eyes! I am a good source of vitamin C and minerals. Do you know that I can be eaten raw, cooked and made into pickles also?

Brinjal

I am the purple-coloured brinjal. I come in different shapes and sizes—big and round or thin and long. I am also known as eggplant. I grow on small plants with tiny thorns. I have a small green cap on my head. I can be cooked in various manners. I have many useful qualities. Some of my cousins are green and white too! Count the different types of brinjals in the picture.

Lady's finger (okra)

I am the slim and delicate lady's finger. My colour is green and I contain lots of tiny white seeds inside. I grow on short plants and have a long green cap on my head. I am not peeled but can be cut into small pieces or fried whole. I am good for your health as I am a rich source of vitamins and fibre.

Spinach

I am dark green and leafy spinach, Popyee's favourite vegetable! When I am fresh and tender, I can be eaten raw in a salad or made into juice. I am also cooked in different ways. I have plenty of minerals and vitamins that help you to be strong and stay healthy.

Beetroot

I am the round and dark red beetroot. I am sweet and crunchy when sliced and added to a salad. I am also cooked as a vegetable, made into juice and pickled. I grow underground. I am an excellent source of vitamins and minerals to keep your blood healthy.

Corn

I am corn. I am also known as maize. I have lots of tiny sweet kernels stuck to my thick centre which is called cob. I am an excellent source of fibre and vitamins. Though the cob is hard, it can be eaten after it has been boiled. I can also be made into a soup. Interestingly, the kernels or seeds of corn are eaten as popcorn! Do you know, I am the favourite of most farm animals?

Peas

I am everyone's favourite peas. I am sweet and delicious to eat when I am young. I am small and grow in a row inside a pod. I grow on a creeper and am the favourite of parrots. I can be eaten raw, after shelling the pods. I am added to various dishes and soups. I am a rich source of minerals that keep you healthy.

Tomato

I am tomato, deep red in colour, soft and round. I look like a fruit but I am thought to be a vegetable. I am made into soup and added to many dishes. I give a nice colour and taste to every dish. Did you know that ketchup is made of tomatoes?

Pumpkin

I am pumpkin. I am a big round ball with lines on my orange skin. I grow on a creeper and my leaves are also eaten. I am tender inside and am eaten either as a tasty vegetable or as soup. My ripe seeds are also eaten as these are rich in several minerals. Do you know that I am used in Halloween? Find out how.

Radish

I am radish. I look like a carrot but I am white and not so sweet. I am eaten in a salad as I am fresh and crunchy to taste. I am also used in cooking. I am an excellent source of useful minerals and vitamins. My leaves can also be eaten. I grow under the ground. Do you know that horses love to eat me?

Lettuce

I am lettuce. I have a pretty pale green colour and come in a bunch of curly, crisp leaves. I am best eaten raw in a salad. I can also be chopped fine, cooked and eaten. I have plenty of vitamins to maintain your good health.

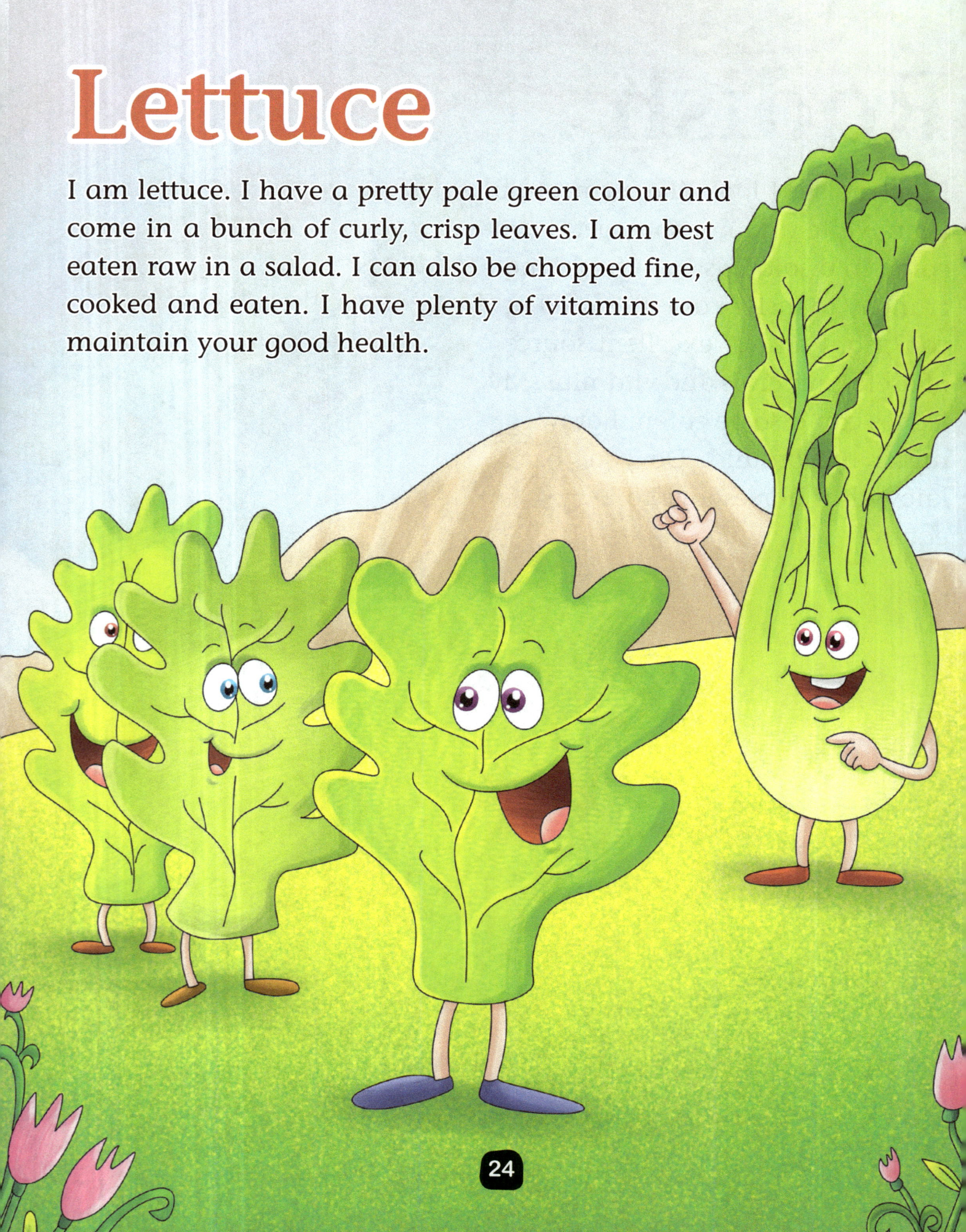

Match the pictures with their names.

Potato

Peas

Tomato

Onion

Cabbage

Carrot

How many vegetables are hidden in the grid?

C	A	R	E	B	S	Z	P
U	G	A	T	R	H	E	U
C	R	D	O	I	W	P	M
U	E	I	I	N	Q	E	P
M	W	S	P	J	A	A	K
B	H	H	L	A	Z	S	I
E	J	Q	E	L	C	X	N
R	E	E	C	O	R	N	E

Circle the green vegetables.

Look at the vegetables below. Circle the vegetables that grow under the ground.

Circle the vegetables that have the same colour.

Vegetable painting.

take a lady's finger or a potato. Ask an adult to cut it in half. Now dip it in colour to make new designs and patterns.

Suggestion: We can have an activity where parent can cut the lady's finger, give to the child to dip in paint and press on paper to see the pattern formed. Using different colours can make attractive patterns. A shape can be cut on potato and same colour printing can be done.